doggie days love guide

GERMAN SHEPHERD

Other Doggie Days Products:

Wall Calendars

Doggie Days Beagle
Doggie Days Dachshund
Doggie Days German Shepherd
Doggie Days Golden Retriever
Doggie Days Jack Russell Terrier
Doggie Days Labrador Retriever
Doggie Days Rottweiler
Doggie Days West Highland Terrier

Dated Engagement Calendars

Doggie Days

Books

Doggie Days Love Guide for Golden Retrievers
Doggie Days Love Guide for Beagles
Doggie Days Love Guide for Labrador Retrievers
Doggie Days Love Guide for German Shepherds

Design and Art Direction by Leslie Evans
Photographs by Shoshannah White for Leslie Evans Design Associates, Inc.

German shepherds courtesy of:
Lebenshunger German Shepherds • Bangor, Maine • 207-942-4999 • www.lebenshunger.com

Published by Ronnie Sellers Productions, Inc.
81 West Commercial Street, Portland, Maine 04101
www.makefun.com, E-mail: rsp@rsvp.com
ISBN: 1-56906-558-6
Printed in China

10 9 8 7 6 5 4 3 2 1

CONTENTS

Introduction

In the world of dogs,
I'm a Genius.
I'm a German Shepherd.
I'm also a HUGE love hound!
I have excellent instincts,
especially when I'm judging people.
This book tells you everything
you need to know
to win my love for life.

CHAPTER 1

What I Look for When I'm Looking for Love

When interviewing prospective owners, my first question always is, "How big is your house?"

My second question? "How big is your yard?"

But really the most important question is, "How big is your heart?"

I'm a good watchdog, so many people think I'm **all business**. But I have my **goofy** side too. I like people who don't take life **too seriously**.

I am an active dog. I have lots of energy. I need two walks a day. If you're a couch potato, I have a suggestion: Get yourself a parakeet!

I'm very affectionate and I'm extremely dedicated. I need a whole lotta love! If you have trouble making commitments, please don't waste my time!

Try on-line dating.

I need plenty of quality time with you. I have **no** use for **workaholics.**

If you think you can leave me alone for more than eight hours, **forgetaboutit!**

I like to get up close and personal, so you'd better not have a problem with . . .

dog breath!

Besides, what makes you think people breath is so fragrant?

"My, what big teeth you have!" people often say.

If you value your shoes, then you'd better keep me well supplied with chew toys.

Chew toys also help to keep my teeth and gums healthy.

I'm as loyal as I am courageous.

I want an owner that I can really look up to.

CHAPTER 2

To Know Me is to Love Me

Many people think

they are dog experts

but they don't

know squat!

I may be sweet, but I'm not petite . . . especially when it comes to feet!

I need to have my nails trimmed often.

Please, have the vet teach you how to trim them correctly.

They're very sensitive!

I'm a real "go getter." You throw something, I'll go get it!

Playing fetch is my favorite way to get exercise. Let's do it every day.

I love to romp and roll . . . and things can get **messy.** I need a **shampoo** and a **bath** once a week . . .

And regular brushings,

or you'll have dust bunnies **the size of beachballs** rolling around your living room.

I play hard, and I burn lots of energy. When it's time to eat, I can really put away some chow.

I need two meals; one in the morning and one at night. Of course a treat or two in between is always appreciated!

I like having a **private** place that I can call **my own**.

It doesn't have to be **fancy**, just **comfortable**.

Being a **fearless** **watchdog** is tiring.

When I'm on break,

DO NOT DISTURB!

I'm a dog.

Sometimes I pass a

little gas.

Get over it!

Chapter 3:
Love Me Forever

Promise to **care** for me.

Immunization Record

AGE	Date Given	Rabies	Distemper	Hepatitis	Parvovirus	Coronavirus	Parainfluenza	Kennel Cough	Lyme Disease	
WKS										
WKS										
WKS										
WKS										
WKS										
1 YEAR										
2 YEAR										
3 YEAR										
4 YEAR										
5 YEAR										
6 YEAR										
7 YEAR										
8 YEAR										
9 YEAR										
10 YEAR										
11 YEAR										
12 YEAR										
13 YEAR										
14 YEAR										
15 YEAR										
16 YEAR										

In sickness and in health.

Signs that I'm sick and should see the veterinarian

- I'm not as spunky as usual and I withdraw.
- I stop eating and/or decrease the amount of water I drink.
- I have heavy discharge from my eyes or nose.
- I cough excessively or pant without apparent reason.
- I behave in ways that are unusual.
- I show signs of being in pain, such as limping, yelping, or reacting to being touched in certain places.
- I have trouble urinating or eliminating.
- I have diarrhea or vomiting that persists for more than 24-48 hours.
- I shake my head, scratch, or lick myself excessively.

Promise to **shelter** me and **protect** me, and **keep** me from losing my way.

Don't lose your love puppy

- When outside, always keep your dog on a leash.
- Create a fenced play area for your dog if possible.
- Register your dog with your local municipality and make sure to fasten the tag to its collar securely.
- Purchase a separate tag engraved with the dog's name and your name, address and phone number, as well as any important information (i.e. "Not good with kids," or "I am diabetic").
- Tattoo an I.D. number or your name and phone number on the dog's inner thigh
- Have a microchip implanted. Ask your veterinarian for details.

Promise to be **patient** and kind. I want more than anything else to **please** you, but I'm not perfect.

House training

- Begin with paper training. Confine your dog within a space with several layers of paper on the floor.
- Put a small amount of its urine on the paper.
- Once the dog has eliminated on the paper, remove the top layers. The dog's scent will remain.
- Praise the dog when it goes on the paper, but do not punish it when it doesn't. Simply clean up after it with an enzyme cleaner (NOT ammonia) and try again later.
- Place the dog on the paper often until it learns to go there on its own when it needs to eliminate.
- Take your dog outside first thing in the morning, before you go to bed, and at regular intervals in between.
- Begin by taking it to the same spot each time and using the same command such as "go pee."
- Once your dog learns to eliminate outside, begin varying the places that you take it to for that purpose (so he won't become too attached to the original spot).

Help me **learn** to do all the things that good dogs do.

Obedience training

- *Begin as early as possible:* by the time a puppy is 8 to 10 weeks old, it is capable of learning basic commands such as "sit," "down," and "come."
- *Be consistent:* use the same verbal commands every time to avoid confusion, and make sure that you enforce the same rules from day to day.
- *Use positive reinforcement:* Like people, dogs respond better to positive reinforcement than they do reprimands. Use food treats to reward proper responses.
- *Choose the best time and place to train your dog:* if you are using treats to reinforce behavior, schedule your sessions before mealtime. Find a quiet place without distractions.
- *Be assertive and firm:* dogs are pack animals, and must understand that you are "the leader of the pack."
- *Enroll in formal obedience training classes:* every dog, even an older dog, will benefit from obedience training classes that are conducted by trained professionals. Most obedience training schools require dogs to be at least 6 months old.
- *Practice, practice, practice:* take time on a daily basis to reinforce the behaviors you've taught your dog by practicing with him.

And I promise that I will
be your loyal friend . . .
for all the days
of my life.

4

Love Journal

Who Am I?

My name is:

I was born on:

My mother's name is:

My father's name is:

I came from kennel

I came from a litter of sisters and brothers:

I was adopted on:

What Do I Like?

Favorite Toys:

Favorite Walks:

Favorite Pals:

Favorite Humans:

Favorite Treats:

Favorite Things To Do:

Funniest Habits:

Who Takes Care Of Me

My Veterinarian:

My Groomer:

My Dog Sitter:

My Trainer:

Others:

Memories

Memories

Memories

Memories